RANDOLPH saves CHRISTMAS

Pat Hornsby Crochet
Illustrated by Sarah Gramelspacher

PELICAN PUBLISHING COMPANY

GRETNA 2018

The word "Pelican" and the depiction of a pelican are trademarks of Pelican Publishing Company, Inc., and are registered in the U.S. Patent and Trademark Office.

Library of Congress Cataloging-in-Publication Data

Names: Crochet, Pat Hornsby, author. | Gramelspacher, Sarah, illustrator.
Title: Randolph saves Christmas / Pat Hornsby Crochet ; illustrated by Sarah Gramelspacher.
Description: Gretna : Pelican Publishing Company, 2018. | Summary: Resets the tale of Rudolph the Red Nosed Reindeer in the Louisiana swamp as Randolph, a coon dog puppy scorned for his overly loud bark, saves the day when Santa gets lost. Includes glossary of French words.
Identifiers: LCCN 2018000384| ISBN 9781455622696 (hardcover : alk. paper) | ISBN 9781455622702 (ebook)
Subjects: | CYAC: Barking—Fiction. | Dogs—Fiction. | Santa Claus—Fiction. | Christmas—Fiction. | Swamps—Fiction. | Louisiana—Fiction.
Classification: LCC PZ7.1.C7468 Ran 2018 | DDC [E]—dc23
LC record available at https://lccn.loc.gov/2018000384

Printed in Malaysia

Published by Pelican Publishing Company, Inc.
1000 Burmaster Street, Gretna, Louisiana 70053
www.pelicanpub.com

For my grandkids: Kate, Aven,
Gabriel, Jonah, Jacob, and Olivia
May they never stop believing in
the magic of Christmas

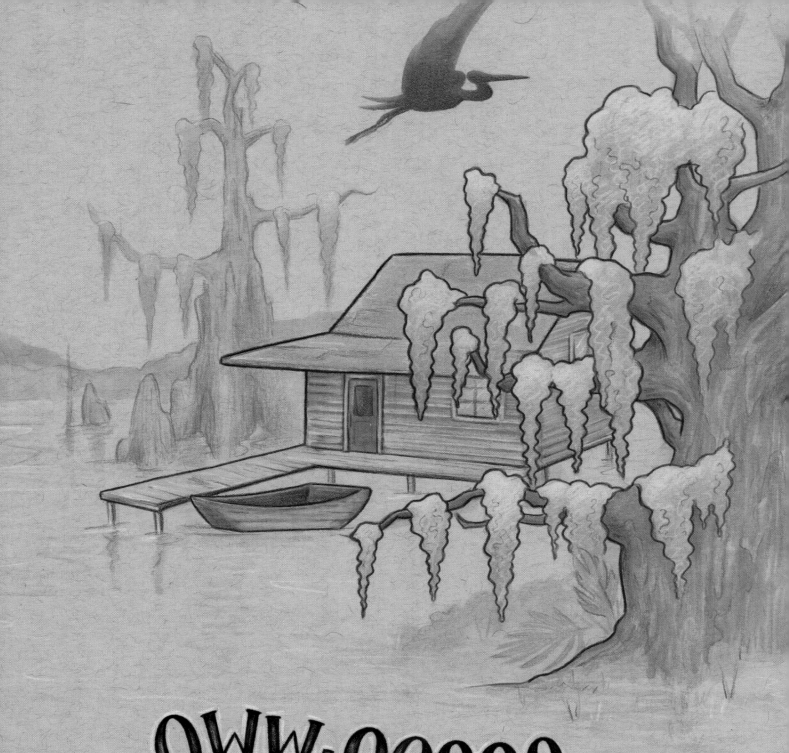

OWW-OOOOO

All up and down the bayou, the noise bounces off mossy trees. It sails over swamp mud as thick as gumbo. It bumps up against pirogues tied to gray wooden docks. The howl plays hide and seek under cabins set high above the ground.

Sac-a-lait mama fish lead their families to the bottom of the lake. That's so the noise won't scare their little sac-a-lait babies. Possums flip over to play dead. Little green alligators turn white with fright.

OWWWWW-OOOOOOO

Turtles pull their heads in. Crawfish scoot backwards into their cozy holes. Raccoons climb the nearest tree.

Over in Nonc Pierre's yard, the sound is cover-
your-ears loud. Chickens scurry into the coop
and slam the door shut. Coonhound puppies
rub their ears with their paws.

Out in the middle of the yard sits the
source of the yowling. As coonhounds
go, he is not big, but he has the
biggest bark on the bayou.

"Randolph!" Mama Coonhound barks.
The noise stops.

"He woke us up," says one droopy-faced coonhound pup.

"My ears hurt!" complains another.

"Mama, make him stop doing that!" Randolph's brothers and sister plead.

"I'm sorry," says Randolph. He hangs his head. "I don't mean for it to be that loud. I promise I won't do it ever again."

The other puppies roll on the ground laughing. Randolph *always* says he's sorry. And he *always* promises it won't happen again. But every morning, there he goes again.

"Now, pups, Randolph says he sorry."

Randolph nods.

"And he won't do it again. Will you, Randolph?"

Randolph shakes his head. His ears flop as only a coonhound's ears can.

"Tomorrow's Christmas," says Angelique, the smallest of the coonhound pups. "If he barks that loud, he's going to scare Santa Claus away."

The others nod in agreement. Randolph hangs his head and trots away.

Mama calls after him. "Randolph, don't you want breakfast?"

"*I'm not* . . . ," he starts, " . . . hungry," he finishes in a little voice.

Randolph goes deep into the swamp. He crawls into a favorite place, under a huge elephant-ear plant.

Now no one can hear me if I bark too loud, Randolph thinks. He curls into a little ball and falls asleep.

All that Christmas Eve, Randolph sleeps and dreams. As the light begins to fade, a low fog hangs over the swamp. Randolph's growling tummy wakes him up. It must be time for supper!

Then, he hears bells jingle. Feet stomp. A big animal snorts. Randolph peeks out between the cypress-tree knees. An old man with a long white beard and a red suit mutters over a huge map. He glances up. He shakes his head, then looks down at the map again. Nearby are a team of reindeer and an odd-looking boat.

Randolph thinks he's still dreaming. He rubs his eyes.

The old man is still there. And so are the reindeer. And the boat thing doesn't look anything like the pirogue Nonc Pierre uses to travel up and down the bayou. Randolph leans closer to get a better look.

PLOP!

He falls at the man's feet.
"Ho-ho-ho. What do we have here?"
Randolph just stares.
"Speak up, pup. Who are you?"
"I'm Randolph. Who are *youuuuu?*"
"Oh, my. Such a big voice for such a little pup."
Embarrassed, Randolph hangs his head and turns to go.

"Wait a minute." The man grabs Randolph by the scruff of his neck and lifts him off the ground.

Randolph's feet paw the air. "I gotta go home. It's suppertime and I'm *soooo hungry.*"

The old man thinks and snaps his fingers. "Where do you live?"

"Near Montegut. Just far enough away from here that my family can't hear my barking."

The man sets Randolph down. He strokes his long white beard. Then he says, "I'm afraid we're lost. Rudolph had a terrible cold and couldn't come with me. I have this map. But I spilled café au lait on it when we took a sharp turn at Des Allemands. Now I can't tell Petit Caillou from Thibodaux." He turns the map upside down and sideways. He squints his eyes at it.

Randolph says, "Well, Montegut is just a holler away from here. So Petit Caillou is real close, a hoot and holler away, like my mama says."

"You know the way, then?"

Randolph nods.

"My problem is solved. You can bark that wonderful loud bark as you go home. Then we can just follow you out!"
"Let's *goooo,*" Randolph answers.

OOOWWW-OOOOO

With a jingle and a jangle and a loud *ho-ho*, the sleigh zooms off. It follows the happy barking of Randolph the Loud-Mouthed Coonhound.

Back in Nonc Pierre's yard, Mama paces back and forth. The coonhound pups lie in a row, their heads on their paws.

All at once Angelique, Bernie, and Marc sit up and lift their ears.

OWWW-OOOOOOO

"It's Randolph!" yips Angelique. "I'd know that howl anywhere."

Randolph trots from the swamp. Their welcome-back barks stop when they see what's following him. The pups stare. Mama gapes. Stomping on the cool damp earth are reindeer. They're the kind that Southern pups only see in books. Behind them is a huge sleigh. It is piled high with toys of every sort.

The driver is a white-bearded old man. He has a twinkle in his eye and a smile on his lips. He jumps down. Then he tosses treats and a tennis ball to each pup.

"We never would have gotten out of that swamp without Randolph's help. That loud voice really came in handy." The man winks. "We're off. We have a lot of deliveries to make before morning."

The man waves to the coonhound family and flies off. He calls out, *"Joyeux Noël* to all!"

"Papa Noel," whispers Angelique.

"Yep," says Randolph, "and *he* likes my loud barking."

"So do we," replies Bernie. "At least when we're not sleeping."

Mama and the pups laugh.

They all join in the coonhound serenade.

Randolph the Loud-Mouthed Coonhound

Randolph the Loud-Mouthed Coonhound
Barked so loud both night and day.
You could even hear him yowling
From Montegut to Point Barré.

All of the other coonhounds
Covered ears when Randolph bayed.
None of them would ever join him
In his coonhound serenade.

Then one murky Christmas Eve
Santa's sleigh was lost
In the swamp near Pointe-aux-Chenes;
He must get out at any cost.

Then came a joyful barking
As Randolph led the reindeer out.
Randolph the Loud-Mouthed Coonhound
Saved the day without a doubt.

Glossary

café au lait (caf-ay oh lay): coffee with milk

Joyeux Noël (zh-why-euh no-ell): Merry Christmas (in French)

murky (murr-kee): foggy

Nonc (nonk): Uncle (in Cajun French)

Papa Noel (papa no-ell): Santa Claus (in French)

pirogue (pee-rohg): small flat-bottomed boat

sac-a-lait (sock-ah-lay): a type of fish

serenade (sare-uh-nayd): a song sung in the open air

Place Names

Des Allemands (dehz ahl-munz)

Montegut (mon-tuh-gyoo)

Petit Caillou (puh-tee k-eye-yoo): a local name for the town of Chauvin (sho-van)

Pointe-aux-Chenes (point-oh-shen)

Point Barré (point bah-ray)

Thibodaux (tib-uh-doh)

Author's Note

The swamps of South Louisiana are home to the many animals mentioned in this story. Rudolph the Red-Nosed Reindeer, made famous by the Christmas TV special and the song sung by Burl Ives, is very much like this story's hero. Like Rudolph, Randolph the Loud-Mouthed Coonhound changes from a source of laughter to his animal companions into a hero who saves Christmas for children—and puppies—waiting for Santa Claus to arrive.